EARLY SKILLS LIBRARY

community awareness

D1404671

Developed by Macmillan Educational Company
Written by Laurie Steding
Text illustrated by Eleanor Wasmuth
Educational Consultant—Marilyn LaPenta
Cover illustrated by Patrick Girouard

Newbridge Educational Programs

TABLE OF CONTENTS

TABLE OF CONTENTS
Continued

EXPLORING THE ENVIRONMENT
Observation Activity

This activity will help children become more aware of their surroundings.

You need: worksheet on page 6
pencils or crayons

Steps:

1. Make a copy of the worksheet on page 6 for each child.

2. Tell the children that they will be taking a walk outside to observe their surroundings. Then read the directions on the worksheet to the class, asking children to listen carefully so that they know what to look for on their walk.

3. Take the class outside and let children walk around the playground and school or in the neighborhood. Encourage them to use their different senses as they observe.

4. After about 10 minutes, take the class back to the classroom.

5. Give each child a worksheet and a pencil or some crayons. Have children complete their worksheets.

6. Discuss the different things the children saw, heard, and smelled on their walk outside. Make a list on the chalkboard of these objects.

Variations:

1. With younger classes, go for a walk outside. Every few minutes, stop the children and give them instructions. (For example: "Look up. What do you see?" "Look down. What do you see?") Each time, call on four or five different children to respond. Ask children to look for objects of specific colors, shapes, and sizes.

2. Divide a class of older children into groups of four or five students each. Make a list of things for each group to look for on their walk. Each group's list should be different. Ask children to look for things of various colors, materials, shapes, sizes, and so on.

Name_____

1. Find three things that are alive. Write their names or draw pictures of them in this space.

_____

_____

_____

2. Find three things that are not alive. Write their names or draw pictures of them in this space.

_____

_____

_____

3. Listen for a sound. In this space, write the name or draw a picture of the thing that made the sound you heard.

_____

4. Use your nose to smell. In this space, write the name or draw a picture of something you smelled.

_____

MAN-MADE OR NATURAL?
Classification Activity

This activity teaches children to distinguish between objects created by humans and those that exist naturally in our environment.

You need: old magazines with colorful pictures
scissors
glue
9″ × 12″ oaktag
dark marker
pushpins

Steps:

1. Look through old magazines to find colorful pictures of man-made objects and natural objects or living things. Try to find fifteen pictures for each category. Avoid choosing pictures that show both natural and man-made objects, or those that show the natural materials that have been shaped by humans (stone sculptures, wooden furniture, and so on).

2. Cut out the pictures and glue each one onto a 9″ × 12″ piece of oaktag. Place the pictures on a desk or table near a bulletin board.

3. Using a dark marker, make two oaktag labels, one reading "man-made" and the other "natural." Pin one label onto the left-hand side of a bulletin board and the other onto the right-hand side.

4. Explain to children that people have made many of the things around us, but that some things have been created by nature.

5. Let the children go one at a time, to the desk or table and select a picture. Ask each child to tell the class what the picture shows and whether the pictured object is man-made or natural. The child will then pin the picture beneath the correct label on the bulletin board. Encourage children to discuss each picture, how it can be used, and so on.

Follow-up Activities:

1. Let children make their own books, entitled *Man-made or Natural?* Give each child two pieces of typing paper. Have each child fold the papers in half widthwise and put one inside the other with the folds at the left. Next, ask each child to look through old magazines to find three pictures of man-made objects and three of natural objects. Have the children cut out the pictures and paste them inside their books. Have children label each picture "man-made" or "natural" and then write the title on the front of their books. Staple the books' pages together along the folds.

2. Have a "Man-made or Natural" scavenger hunt. Divide the class into several small groups. Give each group a paper bag and take them outside. Ask the groups to collect several small man-made and natural objects. Discuss each group's objects when you return to the classroom.

The trash-gobbler puppet and game will help children learn that it is important
for people to dispose of trash properly.

TRASH-GOBBLER PUPPET

You need: 6″ white paper plates (two for each puppet)
fine-line markers or crayons
glue
odds and ends: buttons, pipe cleaners, bits of yarn,
 construction-paper scraps, and so on
stapler

Steps:

1. Make several trash-gobbler puppets to use in the game described on this page. Prepare one puppet for every four or five children in your class.

2. To make the puppet's head, turn a 6″ white paper plate upside down and decorate it outlandishly with fine-line markers or crayons. Draw on goofy-looking eyes and a funny nose. Do not make a mouth for the puppet here. Glue odds and ends like pipe cleaners and yarn scraps onto the puppet's head to make hair. Let children help design the trash gobbler's head.

3. Use another 6″ paper plate to make the trash gobbler's mouth. Color the inside of the plate red. If desired, draw a colorful tongue inside the mouth, as shown.

4. Fold the mouth in half so that the colored area is on the inside. Then place the folded mouth under the puppet's head, aligning the upper curved edge of the folded mouth with the rim of the puppet's head. See illustration.

5. Staple the upper curved edge of the mouth onto the puppet's head, as shown. To open and close the trash gobbler's mouth, the child will slide four fingers of one hand between the folded edge of the mouth and the head, using the thumb to move the lower part of the puppet's mouth.

TRASH-GOBBLER RELAY

You need: masking tape
old newspapers crumpled into balls
brown-paper grocery bags (one for each team)
trash-gobbler puppets (one for each team)

Steps:

1. Divide the class into equal teams of four or five children each.

2. Place a long strip of masking tape on the floor in an open area of the classroom.

3. Scatter many balls of crumpled newspaper in front of the masking-tape strip. (Make at least one newspaper ball for each child in the class, more if possible.)

4. Ask each team to line up behind the strip of tape. Place a brown-paper grocery bag on the floor in front of each team. Then give the first child on each team a trash-gobbler puppet.

5. At the starting signal, the first player on each team will cross the strip of tape and grab a newspaper ball with the trash-gobbler puppet. He or she then runs to the team's grocery bag and drops the newspaper ball into it. The player hands the puppet to the next child before going to the end of the team's line.

6. Each child in turn takes the puppet, picks up a newspaper ball in its mouth, and drops the ball into the grocery bag. Players continue the game until all of the newspaper balls have been picked up.

7. At the end of the game, count the newspaper balls in each team's bag. The team that collected the most balls is the winner.

MOLDED RELIEF MAPS
Art Activity / Dough Recipe

This activity familiarizes children with various natural and man-made landmarks.

SALT-FLOUR RELIEF MAPS

You need: 18″ × 18″ pieces of heavy cardboard (one for each group)
pencils
salt-flour dough (see recipe on this page)
fine-line markers
1″ × 3″ strips of colored construction paper
tape
toothpicks
various colors of tempera paints
paintbrushes

Steps:

1. Divide the class into groups of three or four children each. Tell the children that they are going to make maps. They may draw maps of real towns or cities, of the countryside, or of imaginary places.

2. Give each group a piece of 18″ × 18″ heavy cardboard. Have children work together to plan the scene they will create. Ask children to draw streets, buildings, streams, and lakes on the cardboard with pencils.

3. Give each child a fistful of dough and ask him or her to build a shape to go on the map, placing the dough directly on the board. Children may mold the dough into mountains, houses, riverbanks, or any other shapes they choose.

4. Before the shapes dry, children may want to name the places they have molded. They can make labels for the various places by writing the names on 1″ × 3″ strips of colored construction paper with fine-line markers and taping them onto toothpicks to make flags. The flags can then be inserted into the wet dough.

5. After the children have finished building and labeling their maps, let the maps dry for two or three days.

6. When the dough has dried, children can paint the shapes and drawn-on landmarks with tempera paints. If desired, children may glue sand or Easter grass onto the maps for decoration.

7. Let each group of children tell about the map they made, pointing out the various landmarks.

SALT-FLOUR DOUGH

Ingredients: 2 cups salt
2 cups baking soda
2 cups flour
2½ cups water

How to Make:

1. In a large bowl, mix together salt, baking soda, and flour.

2. Slowly add the water as you stir the mixture. The mixture should be wet and pliable but not runny. (Makes 20 fist-sized balls of dough.)

The pictures below are all mixed up.
They tell the story of Betsy Bear and her lost doll.
The first picture has been labeled for you.
Read the sentence labels at the right of the page.
Cut them out and paste each label in the space below the correct picture.
Then cut out the pictures and put them in order. Staple them together to make a minibook.

Name _____

1. Betsy Bear lost her doll one day.

2. Betsy looked <u>on top of</u> the table for her lost doll.

3. She looked <u>next to</u> the chair for her lost doll.

4. Betsy looked <u>in back of</u> the plant for her lost doll.

5. Hurray! Betsy found her doll <u>in front of</u> the door.

6. That night, Betsy put her doll to bed <u>under</u> the blanket.

Discussion / Class Mural

This activity will help children learn that many aspects of our lives change as time passes.

TODAY AND TOMORROW

Discussion:

1. Have children describe the world they live in today. Ask the class the following questions: What kind of building do you live in? How do you get from place to place? What do you do after school? On the weekends? What kind of clothes do you wear?

2. Ask children to imagine what life will be like when they are grown up. Will the world have changed much? What will be different?

3. Ask children if they have ever seen a movie or a TV show about the future. Have them describe some differences between that future life and our life today.

4. Next, have children talk about some changes they think may take place in the future. Will buildings change? How? What about cars, planes, trains, buses? What kind of clothing will people wear? What things will they do in their spare time?

FUTURELAND MURAL

You need: white butcher paper
tempera paints
aluminum pie pans
paintbrushes
scissors
odds and ends: fabric and yarn scraps, aluminum foil,
  colored tissue paper, wallpaper, and gift wrapping scraps
glue
markers
construction paper of various colors
thumbtacks or pushpins

Steps:

1. Divide the children into three groups.

2. Group 1 will create a background for the mural. Provide these children with paintbrushes and different colors of tempera paints in aluminum pie pans. On a large sheet of butcher paper that is slightly smaller than your bulletin board, have the children paint the landscape, sky, water, and plant life.

3. Group 2 will design the buildings and transportation of the future by cutting scraps of colored paper, aluminum foil, wallpaper, and gift wrapping, and gluing them onto the mural. Children can use markers to decorate the buildings and vehicles.

4. Have group 3 create the people and animals of the future by cutting them from construction paper and gluing on scraps of fabric, yarn, wallpaper, and tissue paper for clothing or fur. The people and animals can be glued on to complete the mural after the background has been created and the buildings and vehicles are in place.

5. Attach the mural to the bulletin board with thumbtacks or pushpins. Have children talk about their mural, describing what the people and animals are doing, how the different vehicles work, and what the environment is like.

Variation:

After the class discussion "Today and Tomorrow," instead of making the "Futureland" mural, let each child draw a picture of an object or living thing that may exist in the future. Post the children's drawings on a bulletin board.

Let children put on their own "fashion show" to reinforce the concept that people need different kinds of clothes for different kinds of weather.

You need: clothing catalogs or magazines
scissors
paste
9″ × 12″ oaktag

Steps:

1. Give each child a clothing catalog or magazine.

2. Ask each child to cut out a picture of a piece of clothing he or she likes.

3. Have the child paste the picture onto a piece of oaktag.

4. When all the children have cut out the pictures and mounted them on oaktag, ask a child to show his or her picture to the class. Have the child name the article of clothing and tell what kind of weather it can be worn in—cold, warm, rainy, or any weather.

5. Let each child describe the weather for which his or her article of clothing is best suited. Children can then discuss the various possibilities for wearing the clothing.

Variation:

Collect a variety of children's clean, old clothing and accessories (hats, sweaters, T-shirts, shorts, sunglasses, umbrellas, mittens, sandals, and so on). Store in a large cardboard box. Put on a live "fashion show" by having each child select an article of clothing or accessory and either wear it or hold it up for classmates to see. Each child can describe the item and tell when it can be worn.

Follow-up Activity:

Have children make booklets showing pictures of clothes for all seasons. Each child will cut several pictures of clothing from old magazines or catalogs. He or she must try to find two types of clothing for each of the following categories: rainy weather, hot weather, and cold weather. Have each child paste the pictures onto pieces of paper, using a separate paper for each category. Children will then staple their papers together to make booklets.

FIND THE POT OF GOLD
Game

This game will help to reinforce different direction words such as
left, right, forward, backward, behind, in front of.

You need: pencil
writing paper
saucepan with cover
small individually wrapped
pieces of butterscotch candy

Steps:

1. Play this game with your class on or near St. Patrick's Day. In advance, plan where to hide the "pot of gold" in your classroom (in a closet, behind a stack of books, in a drawer or cabinet). Then make several different sets of simple directions for teams of children to follow. Write each set of directions in pencil on separate sheets of writing paper. Each set should contain four or five steps, including a starting point for the team of searchers. For example:

   a. Stand in front of the sink.
   b. Turn left and walk to the window.
   c. Turn right and walk to the math table.
   d. Walk forward three steps from the math table.
   e. Look behind the books on the shelf.

2. To make the pot of gold, fill a saucepan partway with small individually wrapped pieces of butterscotch candy (two pieces of candy for each child). Place the cover on the saucepan and hide the pan in the classroom.

3. Divide the class into teams of three or four children each. Give each team a set of directions.

4. At the starting signal, each team will read and follow the directions to find the pot of gold.

5. The team that finds the pot of gold will pass out one or two pieces of candy to each child in the class.

Variations:

1. For younger children, give the directions orally. Have one team at a time close their eyes and put their heads down while you hide the pot of gold. Then have the children raise their heads and open their eyes. Give the directions one at a time. Repeat with the other teams, hiding the pot of gold in a different place each time.

2. Play this game at Halloween. Prepare a small trick-or-treat bag for each team and hide the bags in different places around the room. When the teams find their bags, let the children on each team share the treats.

INSIDE, OUTSIDE
Worksheet

Fold a blank piece of paper in half lengthwise.
Turn the folded paper so that the folded edge is at the left.
Next, look at each picture on this page.
If a picture shows something that you do <u>inside</u> your home, cut it out and paste it onto the <u>inside</u> of your folded paper.
If a picture shows something that you do <u>outside</u> your home, cut it out and paste it onto the <u>outside</u> of your folded paper.

Name _____

A PLACE FOR EVERYTHING
Worksheet

Look at the two pictures below.
The left-hand picture shows five objects that are out of place.
The right-hand picture shows the five objects in the correct places.
In the picture on the left, draw circles around the five objects that are out of place.

Name _____

This activity teaches children that families are made up of individuals, and that each family is unique.

You need: 12″ × 18″ white construction paper
crayons
writing paper
pencils
thumbtacks or pushpins

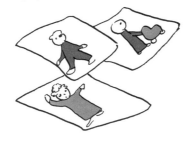

Steps:

1. Give each child a 12″ × 18″ piece of white construction paper and some crayons.

2. Ask children to draw pictures of their family members on their papers.

3. Each child will then write or dictate two or three sentences about his or her family—what jobs the different family members do around the house, what they enjoy doing together as a family, what the individual family members like to do.

4. Have each child show his or her picture to the class and tell about his or her family. Then display the children's pictures and sentences on a bulletin board.

Variations:

1. Children may bring in individual photographs of each of their family members and paste them onto pieces of 9″ × 12″ white construction paper to make family collages. Display the collages along with the children's sentences on a bulletin board.

2. Have children cut out several pictures of adults and children from magazines or catalogs. Ask children to paste the pictures onto oaktag to make "paper doll" figures. Children may use these figures to dramatize family activities and events.

This game will help reinforce children's recognition of traffic signs and understanding of safety rules.

You need: game cards on this page and game board
  on page 18
  glue
  oaktag
  scissors
  red, yellow, and green markers
  small objects to use as playing
    pieces (buttons, coins, paper clips)

Optional: clear plastic adhesive

Steps:

1. Make four copies of the game cards on this page and one copy of the game board on page 18.

2. Glue the cards and game board onto oaktag and cut them out along the dotted lines.

3. Use red, yellow, or green markers to color in one circle on each traffic-light card. Make four cards showing red lights, four with yellow lights, and four with green lights.

4. Next, laminate the cards and game board or cover with clear plastic adhesive.

5. Shuffle the cards and place them facedown in a pile next to the game board. Two to four children may play this game. Give each child a small object to use as a playing piece (e.g., button, coin, or paper clip). Have children place their pieces on the house marked HOME on the game board.

6. Explain that the boxes on the game board represent sidewalks. Each player must move his or her piece from HOME to SCHOOL, staying on the sidewalks and crossing the streets only at the corners. Players may move along any route they choose. To cross a street, a player must draw a card showing a green light, a crossing guard, or a "walk" sign. If the child draws a red light, yellow light, or "don't walk" sign, he or she loses the turn. A player may move his or her piece only once during a turn.

7. Let the youngest child begin. The player may choose to move his or her piece one space along the sidewalk or to draw the top card from the pile and try to cross the street. The player may cross the

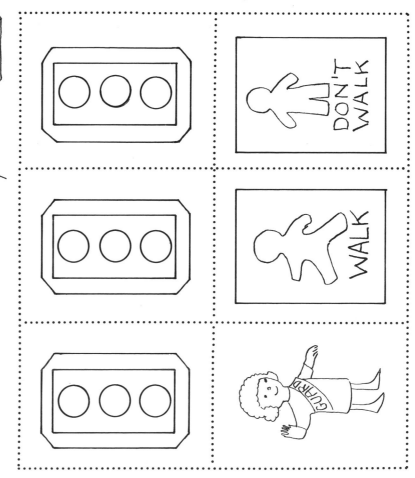

street only if the card drawn shows a green light, a crossing guard, or a "walk" sign. The card is then placed faceup next to the card pile.

8. The game continues clockwise, each player moving his or her piece one space along the sidewalk or crossing a street at a corner after drawing an appropriate card. If there are no more cards left in the pile, the discarded cards may be shuffled and turned facedown. The first player to reach the school is the winner.

CROSS WITH CARE!
Game Board

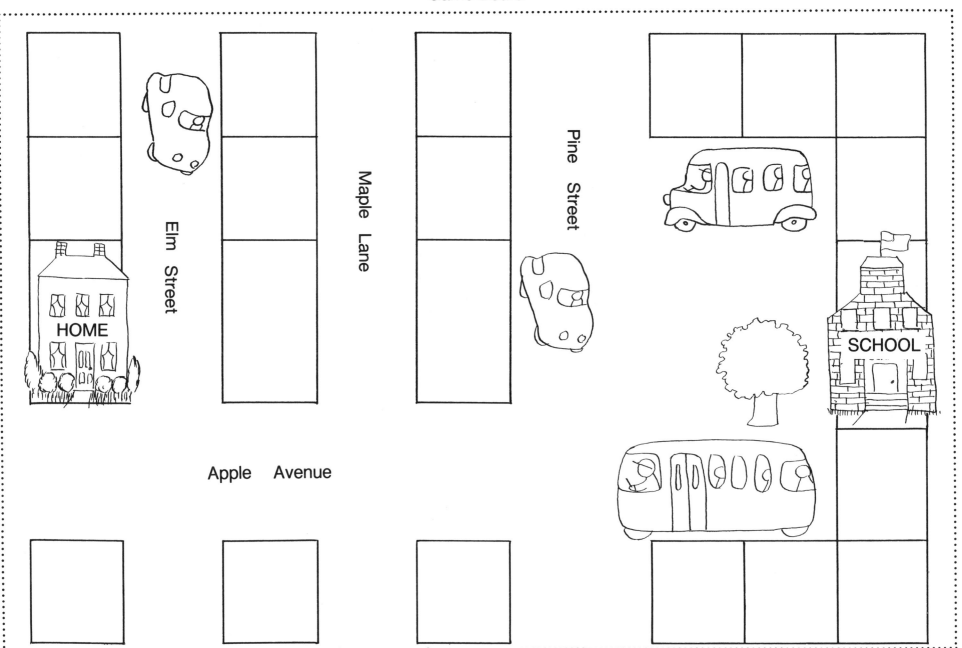

Use this play to teach children how family members and/or neighbors can be of help to each other in the community. Make the props on pages 21 and 22 to use with this play. Let students stage the play for their classmates, other classes, or parents.

Characters:

First Little Pig
Second Little Pig
Third Little Pig
Narrator
Straw Salesperson
Stick Salesperson
Brick Salesperson
Wolf

(The play begins with the three little pigs standing together on the stage.)

NARRATOR: Once upon a time there were three little pigs who were all alone in the world. They all needed places to live.

FIRST PIG: What can I use to build a nice house?

(STRAW SALESPERSON enters.)

STRAW SALESPERSON: Straw here! Straw for sale!

FIRST PIG: I think I'll buy some straw to build my house.

(STRAW SALESPERSON and FIRST PIG exit together.)

THIRD PIG: Straw isn't strong enough for *my* house! I'll have to think of something else.

(STICK SALESPERSON enters.)

STICK SALESPERSON: Get your sticks here! Special stick sale today only!

SECOND PIG: Sticks are just what I need to build my house. I'll have my house finished in no time. See you later.

(STICK SALESPERSON and SECOND PIG exit together.)

THIRD PIG: I wonder what I can make my house with?

(BRICK SALESPERSON enters.)

BRICK SALESPERSON: Bricks for sale! Buy your bricks here!

THIRD PIG: Bricks! They're perfect for building my house. I'd better get to work.

(BRICK SALESPERSON and THIRD PIG exit together.)

NARRATOR: The three little pigs worked very hard to build their houses. The first little pig was finished quickly and went to sleep inside the straw house that night.

(FIRST PIG enters, holding straw roof above head. WOLF enters, grinning and licking chops.)

WOLF: Little pig, little pig, let me come in!

FIRST PIG: No! No! Not by the hair of my chinny chin chin!

WOLF: Then I'll huff and I'll puff and I'll BLOW your house down!

(WOLF huffs and puffs. FIRST PIG lowers straw roof from over head and runs off stage squealing. WOLF follows, rubbing hands together.)

NARRATOR: The first little pig ran to the second little pig's house to get help.

(SECOND PIG enters, holding stick roof above head. FIRST PIG runs up to SECOND PIG.)

FIRST PIG: Can I stay with you, little pig? The wolf just blew my house down!

SECOND PIG: Sure. Come on inside. I'm glad I used sticks instead of straw to build *my* house.

(WOLF enters, grinning and licking chops.)

WOLF: Little pigs, little pigs, let me come in!

SECOND PIG: No! No! Not by the hair of my chinny chin chin!

WOLF: Then I'll huff and I'll puff and I'll BLOW your house down!

(WOLF huffs and puffs. SECOND PIG lowers stick roof from over head. The TWO PIGS run off stage, chased by the WOLF.)

NARRATOR: Luckily, the two little pigs got away from the wolf. They ran to the house of the third little pig.

(THIRD PIG enters, holding brick-colored roof over head. FIRST and SECOND PIGS run up to THIRD PIG.)

FIRST PIG: Please help us, little pig! The wolf blew our houses down, and now he's after us!

THIRD PIG: Come in. But hurry! I think I hear someone coming!

(WOLF enters, grinning and licking chops.)

WOLF: Little pigs, little pigs, let me come in!

THIRD PIG: No! No! Not by the hair of my chinny chin chin!

WOLF: Then I'll huff and I'll puff and I'll BLOW your house down!

(WOLF huffs and puffs but nothing happens. The THREE PIGS laugh.)

NARRATOR: The big bad wolf couldn't blow down the house made of bricks, so he decided to come down the chimney instead.

(WOLF pantomimes climbing ladder to the roof.)

SECOND PIG: Uh-oh! I think I hear someone climbing up to the roof.

THIRD PIG: Quick! Let's build a fire so that the wolf can't come down the chimney.

FIRST PIG: You always have the best ideas.

(PIGS pretend to build fire.)

WOLF: I'll just climb down the chimney and surprise those pigs. What's this? Smoke?

(WOLF rubs eyes and coughs.)

WOLF: Those pigs are just too smart for me!

(WOLF stalks off stage angrily.)

SECOND PIG: Hurray! The wolf is gone!

(PIGS join hands and dance in a circle.)

FIRST, SECOND, and THIRD PIGS (chanting):
The big bad wolf is gone,
  Hurray, hurray!
The big bad wolf is gone,
  Hurray, hurray!
Now we can sing and dance all day!
The big bad wolf has gone away!

PIG AND WOLF HEADBANDS

You need: pig and wolf cutouts on page 22
crayons
scissors
stapler
four 2½" × 24" strips of white construction paper

Steps:

1. Reproduce the pig and wolf cutouts on page 22 three times.

2. Color the three pigs and one wolf with crayons, then cut them out. Number the pigs from 1 to 3.

3. Staple each cutout onto the center of a 2½" × 24" strip of white construction paper to make a headband. See illustration.

4. Then staple the ends of each headband together to fit the children's heads.

SALESPEOPLE'S PROPS

You need: small amount of straw
yarn scraps
several thin twigs
brick
9" × 12" oaktag
glue
red crayon

Steps:

1. Make props for the straw, stick, and brick salespeople. Tie a small amount of the straw in a bundle with a scrap of yarn. Do the same with a few of the thin twigs. Let the brick represent the brick salesperson. During the play, each salesperson will hold the appropriate prop.

2. To make the pigs' houses, fold three pieces of 9" × 12" oaktag in half widthwise. Unfold the oaktag pieces and lay them flat, with the inner sections facedown.

3. Spread glue on one piece of oaktag and sprinkle it with straw.

4. On the second piece of oaktag, glue several twigs.

5. With a red crayon, color a bricklike design on the third piece of oaktag. During the play, each little pig will hold the appropriate rooftop in tentlike fashion over his or her head.

6. After the play has been performed, ask children the discussion questions on this page.

Discussion Questions:

1. Can you name what each little pig used to make his home?

2. (Let children lift and compare the salespeople's props.) Which of these materials is lightest? Which is heaviest?

3. Which of these materials made the strongest house? Why?

4. What other materials could the three little pigs have used to build their houses?

5. What is your house or apartment building made of?

CLASSROOM HELPERS
Bulletin-Board Job Roster

Have children help make this bulletin-board display. Use the display to assign various classroom
chores that will teach children how individuals can contribute to the smooth operation
of classroom activities.

You need: 6″ white paper plates
(one for each child)
fine-line markers
rulers
pencils
9″ × 12″ brown construction paper
scissors
stapler
yarn scraps
job cards on page 24

Optional: glue
glitter

Steps:

1. Let children make "hot-air balloons" to decorate the "Classroom
   Helpers" bulletin board. Give each child a 6″ white paper plate and
   have him or her turn it upside down. This is the balloon.

2. Each child will decorate his or her balloon using fine-line markers.
   Encourage children to use stripes, zigzags, polka dots, and other
   designs on the balloons. If desired, children may draw designs with
   glue and sprinkle glitter on the glue.

3. Next, have each child measure and mark a 4″ × 2″ rectangle on
   brown construction paper and cut it out. This is the balloon's
   basket.

4. Each child will turn the basket so that the long sides are horizontal,
   and write his or her name on it with a dark marker.

5. Collect the children's balloons and baskets. Staple a balloon onto a
   bulletin board. Then attach the basket about 4″ below the balloon,
   stapling only along the basket's sides and bottom. Next, staple a
   piece of yarn from each top corner of the basket to each side of the
   balloon, as shown.

6. Do the same with the other balloons and baskets.

7. Reproduce the job cards on page 24 and cut them out. Make
   additional job cards for special chores in your classroom by cutting
   out cards the same size from white construction paper and writing
   job titles on them.

8. At the beginning of each week, slip a job card into each child's
   balloon basket. Children will check the balloons to learn their assigned jobs. Give children new job assignments each week by
   changing the cards in the baskets.

eraser cleaner

chalkboard washer

snack helper

class pet keeper

paper and supply distributor

line leader

plant keeper

toy keeper

art-corner cleaner

At the beginning of the school year, discuss the importance of following rules with your class. Then let children help draft a charter of rules to be followed in the classroom. The class charter can be revised as the need arises throughout the year.

You need: dark marker
large piece of chart paper
crayons
drawing paper
thumbtacks or pushpins

Steps:

1. Open a discussion of rules with children. Ask:

   What rules do you follow when you want to cross a street? Why are these rules important? Can you name any other helpful rules?
   What would happen in our class if everyone talked at the same time? Would we be able to hear what people were saying? What rule could we make so that each person could have a chance to talk while the rest of us listen?

2. Write the rules that children suggest on the chalkboard. Ask children to name other rules that would be helpful in the classroom and list them on the chalkboard. Guide the discussion by suggesting rules or describing situations that could be improved by following rules. For example:

   Raise your hand when you want to speak.
   Walk (don't run) in the classroom.
   Stay in your seat during class.
   Listen when other people are talking.
   Use your own supplies.
   Put your supplies away when you have finished working.
   Talk softly during free time.

   Keep the list fairly short so that children can remember all the rules.

3. Then, using a dark marker, write the rules on a large piece of chart paper under the heading "Class Charter."

4. Post the class charter on a bulletin board.

5. Give each child some crayons and a piece of drawing paper. Ask each child to choose one of the rules and draw a picture of himself or herself following that rule.

6. Post the children's pictures on the bulletin board around the class charter.

7. When necessary, remind the class of specific class-charter rules.

You need: various props (see list of suggested props)

Steps:

1. Have a small group of four to seven children sit in a circle on the floor.

2. Set the props in the center of the circle.

3. Tell the children that they are going to pretend that they are on a shopping trip. Choose one child to begin. He or she selects a prop. The child must state a sentence naming the object and the store where it was purchased. For example: "I bought a pair of shoes at the shoestore."

4. The child to the left of the first child takes the next turn. Choosing a different prop, he or she must repeat the first player's sentence and then add one about the new prop. For example: "I bought a pair of shoes at the shoestore. Then I bought some milk at the grocery store."

5. The game continues clockwise, each player repeating the earlier sentences in sequence and adding a new sentence.

6. A child who forgets the sequence of items purchased must drop out of the game. When two children in a row are unable to list all of the items in sequence, start a new game. Choose a different child to begin the game, and have children put all the props back in the center of the circle.

Suggested props:

shoe store—pair of shoes
grocery store—empty milk carton, empty egg carton
hardware store—hammer, nails, screwdriver
drugstore—empty toothpaste carton, old toothbrush
pet store—pet collar, leash
candy store—empty candy box
plant store—flowerpot
card store—greeting card, notepaper
bookstore—book
post office—empty stamp book
bakery—empty cake box
clothing store—hat, belt, mittens
toy store—stuffed animal, toy car
jewelry store—play necklace or bracelet

Cut out the five signs at the bottom of this page.
Paste them in the correct boxes in the scene below.

Name _____

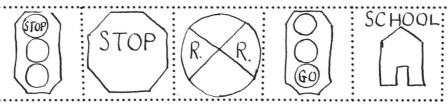

WHAT DO YOU SAY WHEN_____?
Worksheet

Name_____

Read each silly question below. In the blank spaces, write the polite word or words
that answer the question. Use the key at the bottom of the page for extra help.

1. What do you say when you bump into an elephant?

_ _ _ _ _ _ _ _ _ _

2. What do you say when a camel gives you
   a ride on his back?

_ _ _ _ _ _ _ _ _ _ _

3. What do you say when you want to borrow
   a raccoon's mask?

_ _ _ _ _ _ _ _ _ _

4. What do you say when you break a bear's pot of honey?

_ _ _ _ _ _ _ _ _ _ _

5. What do you say when a horse thanks you
   for giving him an apple?

_ _ _ _ _ _ _ _ _

_ _ _ _ _ _ _ _ _

KEY

Thank you.   Please.
You are welcome.   I am sorry.
Excuse me.

This game will familiarize children with different kinds of stores and the goods they provide.

You need: errand cards and game board on
pages 30 and 31
glue
oaktag
scissors
small objects to use as playing
pieces (buttons, beads, paper clips)
die

Optional: clear plastic adhesive

Steps:

1. Reproduce the errand cards and game board on pages 30 and 31.

2. Mount the cards and game board on oaktag and laminate them or cover with clear plastic adhesive. Then cut out the cards.

3. Two to four children may play this game. Give each player a small object to use as a playing piece. The playing pieces are placed on the area marked HOME on the game board.

4. One player shuffles the cards and places them facedown in a pile next to the game board.

5. The object of the game is to be the first player to complete three errands and then return to HOME.

6. The youngest child goes first. To begin the errands, he or she draws the top card from the pile, naming the item pictured and the store where it can be purchased. (For example: "Screwdriver— hardware store.") The child lays the card faceup next to him or her and rolls the die. The player moves his or her playing piece the number of spaces shown toward the appropriate store. He or she may move along the paths in any direction from HOME or another space toward the appropriate store. An exact number is not needed to reach a store.

7. The child to the left of the first player takes a turn, drawing a card, naming the item and appropriate store, and rolling the die to move his or her playing piece. The game continues clockwise.

8. When a player reaches the store where the item shown on the card is sold, he or she takes another card from the top of the pile, turns it faceup, and names the picture and the correct store. If the item shown on the card is found in the store where the player is now, the child must place the card on the bottom of the pile and take another card. The player must wait until his or her next turn before tossing the die and moving toward the new destination.

9. Players may move their pieces in any direction around the board, following the shortest routes to the different stores. A player may toss the die and move his or her playing piece only once during a turn. He or she may not travel to the same store on two consecutive errands but may return to the first store on the third errand.

10. After a player has drawn three cards and completed three errands at the appropriate stores, he or she waits for the next turn to roll the die and move his or her playing piece toward HOME. The first player to return to HOME is the winner.

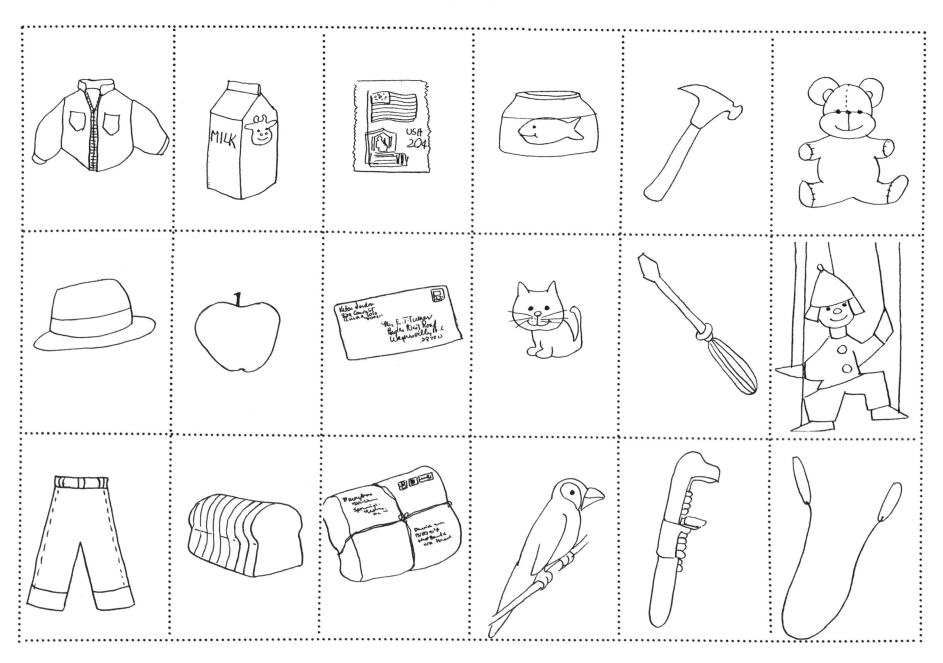

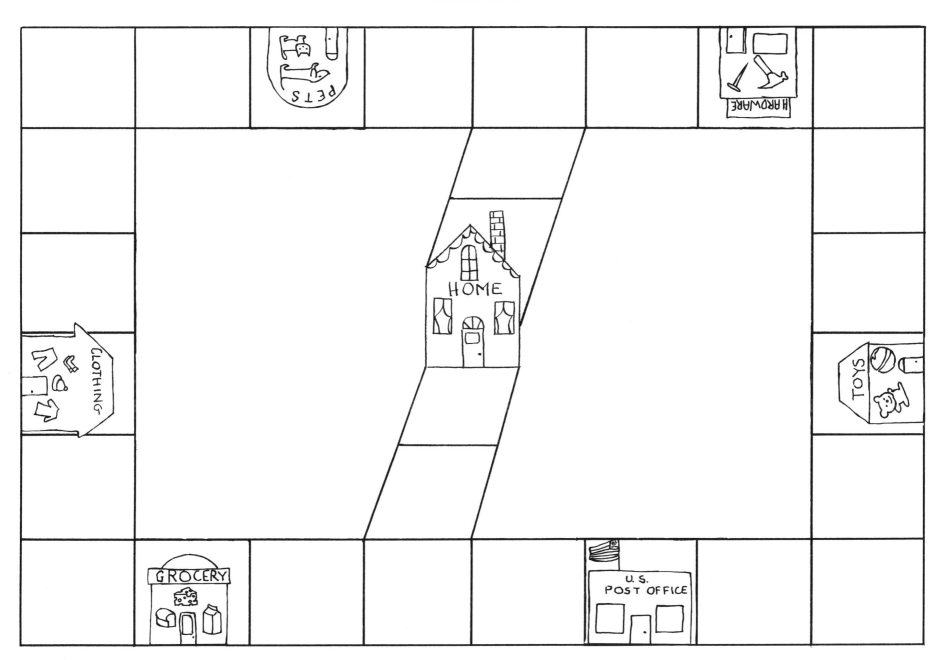

Look carefully at the picture below.
With a green crayon, draw a circle around each vehicle that travels on land.
Use a blue crayon to circle all the vehicles that travel on water.
With a red crayon, draw a circle around each vehicle that travels through the air.

Name _____

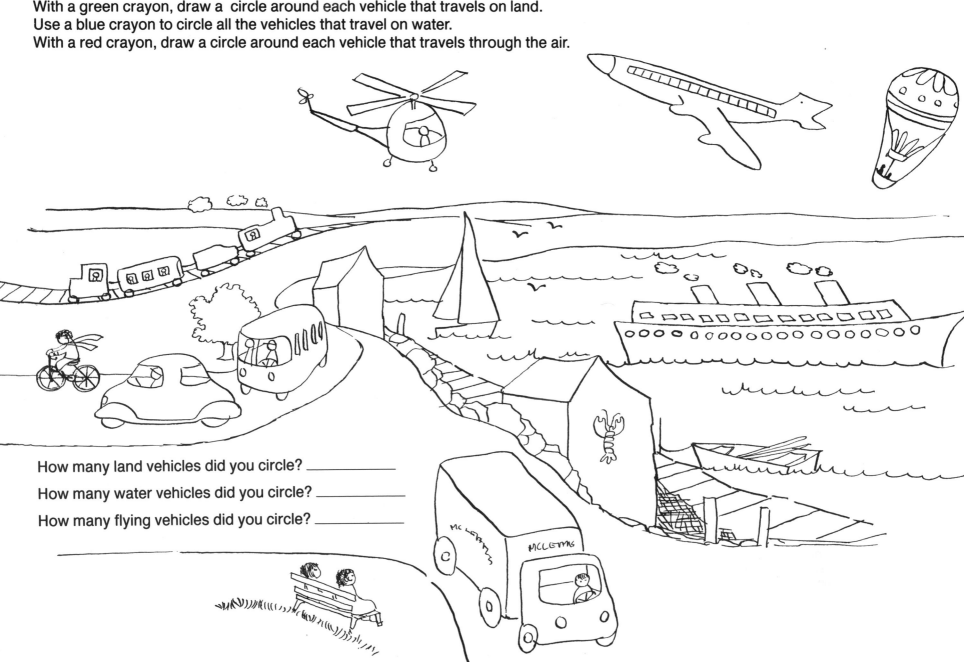

How many land vehicles did you circle? _____

How many water vehicles did you circle? _____

How many flying vehicles did you circle? _____

You need: assortment of clean, empty cardboard and plastic food and beverage containers, e.g., cereal boxes, margarine tubs, egg cartons, frozen-vegetable cartons, juice cartons, and so on
empty bookshelves or bookcase
masking tape
permanent marker
table
two or three shoe boxes
play money
two or three brown paper grocery bags

Steps:

1. Ask children to bring from home empty, clean cardboard and plastic food and beverage containers.

2. Provide empty bookshelves or an empty bookcase in a corner of the room. The shelves should be low enough for children to reach easily.

3. With a piece of masking tape and a permanent marker, make a price tag for each container.

4. Have children work together to arrange the various containers on the shelves.

5. Place a 6′ strip of masking tape on the floor about 5′ in front of the grocery store.

6. Divide the class into two or three equal teams. Select one child from each team to be the cashier. The other children are the shoppers.

7. Have the cashier from each team stand behind the table in the store. Give each cashier a shoe box containing play money and a brown paper grocery bag. Ask the shoppers from each team to line up behind the strip of masking tape. Give each shopper an equal amount of play money.

8. At the starting signal, the first shopper on each team will go into the store and select one item to buy. The child will then take the item to his or her team's cashier and pay for it with play money. The cashier makes change and places the item in the grocery bag. The shopper then takes the place of the cashier, and the cashier goes to the end of the team's line.

9. Have the next player on each team follow the same procedure. Continue until all the players on one team have had turns to be shoppers. The team that finishes first is the winner.

Variations:

1. For older children, write several different shopping lists of five or six items on separate sheets of paper. Place the lists on a table in the grocery store. In their free time, individual children can take a list and collect the items on it. The child will then write the price of each item next to its name on the list and add the prices to show the total cost. After totaling the prices, the child will put the items back on the shelves.

2. Substitute other items in place of the food and beverage containers to create a different kind of store. For example, set up a stationery store with old greeting cards, pads of paper, empty envelope boxes, pencils, and so forth. Supply a toy store with games, dolls, puppets, toy cars, and so on.

OFFICE HOURS OF FUN
Dramatic Play Centers

In their free time, children can act out the roles of doctors and office workers.

DOCTOR'S OFFICE

You need: old magazines
low table or bench
several chairs
desk
play telephone
pad of paper and pencil
play doctor's equipment
 (stethoscope, small hammer,
 blood-pressure band)
shoe box
bandages, tape, and cotton balls
old bathroom scale
scissors
discarded man's shirt (white)
one or two dolls

BUSINESS OFFICE

Steps:

1. Set up a doctor's office in a corner of the room.

2. Place several old magazines on a low table or bench at one end of the play area. Place several chairs around the table or bench. This area is the waiting room.

3. At the other end of the area, set up a desk with a play telephone on it. Put one chair behind the desk and one in front of the desk. Place a pad of paper and a pencil on the desk.

4. Place the play doctor's equipment in a shoe box on the desk. Set bandages, tape, and cotton balls on the desk.

5. Provide an old bathroom scale for the doctor's office. Make a doctor's coat by cutting the sleeves off a discarded man's shirt (white). The child playing the doctor can wear the sleeveless shirt backwards.

6. Let four to six children play in the doctor's office. One child can be the doctor, another the nurse, and the others patients or parents of doll patients.

You need: three or four desks or low tables
three or four chairs
old office equipment: typewriter,
 adding machine
paper and pencils
rubber stamps and stamp pads
two play telephones (or real telephones)

Steps:

1. Set up a business office in one area of the classroom. Place three or four desks or tables and chairs in the area.

2. Put old office machines, paper, pencils, rubber stamps, stamp pads, and play telephones on the desks or tables.

3. Let three or four children at a time play in the office, typing, answering the phones, writing and dictating letters, and stamping papers.

You need: old magazines
scissors
glue
oaktag
9″ × 12″ construction paper
black marker
thumbtacks or pushpins

Optional: clear plastic adhesive

Steps:

1. From old magazines, cut out pictures of 15 to 20 different kinds of food. Make sure to find 2 similar pictures of each item, so that you have a total of 30 or 40 pictures. Be sure to include items from each of the four basic food groups: vegetable and fruit, bread and cereal, milk and meat.

2. Glue one picture of each food item onto oaktag. Then cut out the pictures and laminate them or cover with clear plastic adhesive.

3. Make "menus" for the children to use by folding a 9″ × 12″ piece of construction paper in half widthwise to form a booklet. On the outside cover, write *Menu*. On the inside pages of the menu, glue five or six of the unlaminated pictures of various foods. Prepare several menus in this way.

4. Place the menus on a table near a bulletin board. Pin the laminated food pictures onto the bulletin board.

5. Let groups of three or four children go to the table in their free time. One child will be the waiter or waitress. The other children are the customers. Each customer takes a menu and, in turn, orders one food from the menu. Encourage children to use courtesy words like "please," "thank you," and "you're welcome" when ordering and "serving" the foods. From the bulletin board, the waiter or waitress will remove the picture showing a food similar to the item ordered and give it to the customer.

6. When each customer's order has been filled correctly, the pictures are put back on the bulletin board. Children may play the game again with a different child playing the part of the waiter or waitress.

Variations:

1. Incorporate learning to set a table correctly in this activity. Provide paper plates and cups, napkins, and plastic utensils. Before taking the customers' orders, the waiter or waitress must set their places.

2. For older children, write prices on the menus. The waiter or waitress may write out checks for the customers' orders, and the customers may pay their checks with play money.

You need: picture sets on this page
glue
oaktag
scissors

Optional: clear plastic adhesive

Steps:

1. Reproduce the picture sets on this page.

2. Mount on oaktag and laminate or cover with clear plastic adhesive.

3. Cut out the picture sets and cut each one apart on the dotted line to make puzzle pieces.

4. Mix up the pieces and let individual children put the picture sets together.

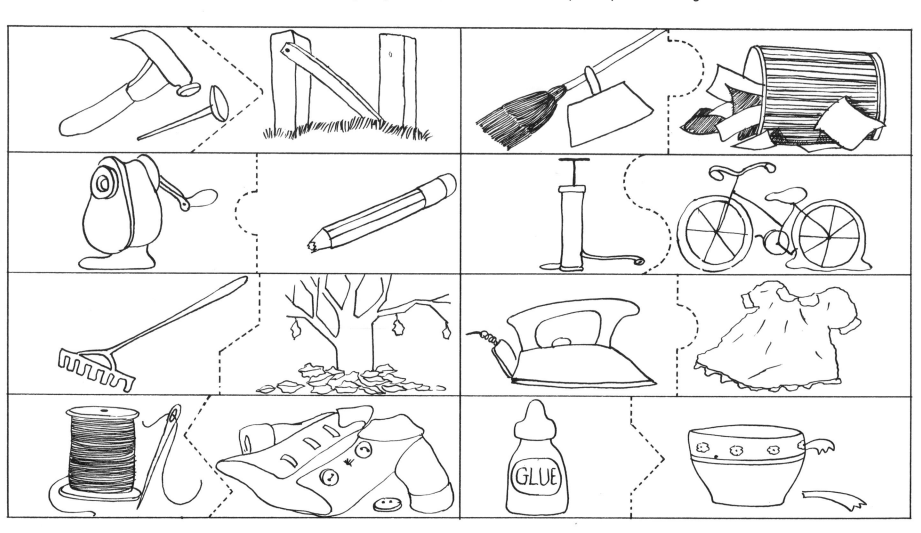

You need: blocks
low table or bench
instrument panel (see instructions on page 38)
four or five chairs
two children's baseball caps
1″ × 3″ strips of scrap paper
hole puncher

Steps:

1. In their free time, groups of four to six children can dramatize traveling by bus, train, or plane.

2. In a corner of the room, have children arrange blocks in a large rectangle on the floor to define the perimeter of the bus, train, or plane.

3. Place a low table or bench at one end of the rectangle. Set the instrument panel on it, and place a chair at the panel.

4. Arrange the remaining chairs in rows inside the rectangle to resemble passenger seats.

5. Select one child to be the driver, engineer, or pilot of the vehicle, and another to be the ticket taker. Give both children caps to wear.

6. The driver takes his or her place at the instrument panel. The ticket taker distributes tickets (1″ × 3″ strips of scrap paper) to the passengers and then uses a hole puncher to validate the tickets.

Variations:

1. Add more passenger seats to the vehicle. Assign two more children the roles of flight attendants or servers. Let them serve the passengers on the plane or train using empty, clean frozen-dinner aluminum trays and paper cups.

2. Have the children plan a pretend trip to a special place (amusement park, beach, national park) and dramatize the journey, telling about what they see as they travel.

INSTRUMENT PANEL

You need: scissors
cardboard box, about 15″ × 11″ × 9″
thick tempera paints and large paintbrush
steering-wheel pattern on page 39
heavy cardboard, at least 12″ square
pencil
paper-towel tube
ruler
masking tape
glue
spray-can cap
several shampoo-bottle caps
thin 6″ dowels
margarine-tub cover, about 4″ in diameter
white construction paper
dark marker
oaktag
brass fastener
old key ring with key attached

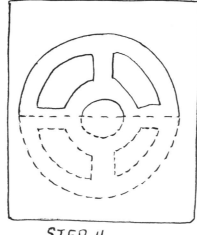

STEP 4

STEP 5   STEP 7

Steps:

1. Cut off the top of a 15″ × 11″ × 9″ cardboard box.

2. Paint the sides and bottom of the box with thick tempera paints. Let dry.

3. Turn the box upside down and set it on a desk or table. This is the base for the instrument panel.

4. Reproduce the steering-wheel pattern on page 39 and cut out. Lay the pattern on a piece of heavy cardboard. Trace the pattern; then flip it over and trace it again, aligning the long straight edge with the first tracing. See illustration.

5. Cut out the cardboard steering wheel and insert one end of the paper-towel tube through the center hole so that the tube protrudes about ½″ past the wheel, as shown. Tape the tube and wheel together securely with masking tape.

6. Glue a spray-can cap over the end of the paper-towel tube in the center of the wheel.

7. Next, cut a 2″ circle in the center of one long side of the instru-

ment panel base and place the tube holding the steering wheel through it, as shown.

8. To make knobs for the panel, glue several shampoo-bottle caps onto the ends of thin 6″ dowels. Cut small holes in the top of the panel and push the free ends of the dowels through them.

9. To make a speedometer, trace a margarine-tub cover (about 4″ in diameter) onto white construction paper. Cut out the circle and mark the miles-per-hour readings, in increments of 5, around the edge. Use a dark marker.

10. Glue the speedometer onto the top of the instrument panel. Then cut an oaktag arrow about 2½″ long and ½″ wide. Attach the arrow to the center of the speedometer with a brass fastener.

11. To the right of the steering wheel, cut a ½″ vertical slit. This is the ignition. Place an old key ring with a key attached next to the instrument panel.

12. The driver starts the vehicle by inserting the key into the ignition. He or she can turn the knobs, move the speedometer's needle, and turn the steering wheel.

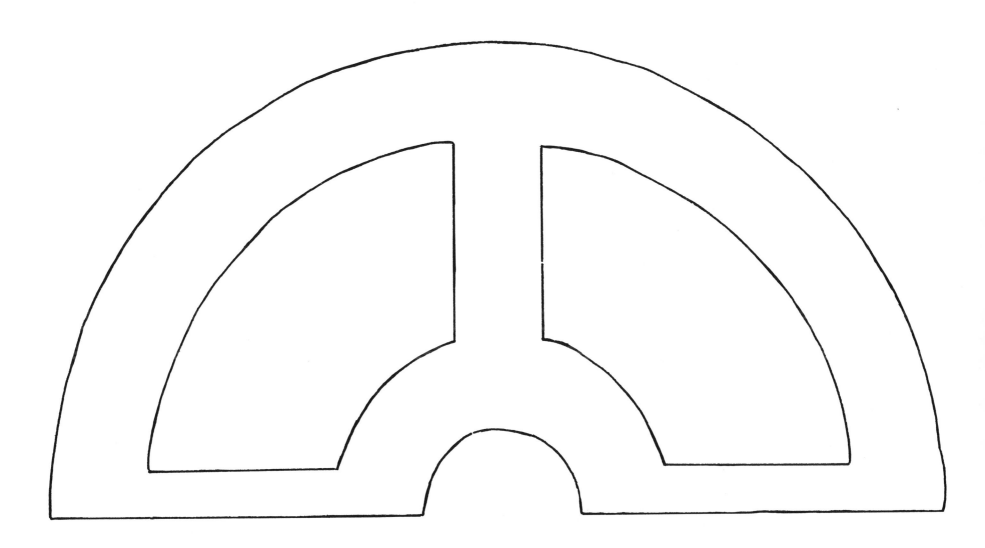

Steps:

1. Read your class the riddles about various machines on this page.

2. After reading each riddle, ask children to raise their hands if they think they know the answer.

3. Call on a child whose hand is raised to give the answer. If children cannot guess the answer, tell them.

Variations:

1. Make this an art activity for older children. Give each child a 9″ × 12″ piece of white construction paper. Ask children to fold their papers into fourths. Children will then unfold their papers and number the boxes on both sides from 1 to 8. Read the riddles to the class, having children draw the answers in the boxes, instead of saying them.

2. Reproduce the riddles on this page and cut them out. Let individual children read the riddles aloud for their classmates to solve.

When you feed me soap and turn me on, I get your clothes clean.
What am I?
(a washing machine)

When you plug me in and turn me on, I help clean your rugs and floors.
What am I?
(a vacuum cleaner)

When you dial my numbers, you can talk to people near and far. And when someone wants to talk to you, I call you with a ring.
What am I?
(a telephone)

When you turn me on, you can hear music or the latest news, but you can't see where these sounds come from.
What am I?
(a radio)

I help you keep your food cold and fresh.
What am I?
(a refrigerator)

I have a screen like a television and keys like a typewriter.
What am I?
(a computer)

When you tap my keys with your fingers, I make words on paper.
What am I?
(a typewriter)

When you use me, I take pictures of people, places, and objects.
What am I?
(a camera)

ASSEMBLY-LINE PARTY FAVORS
Group Activity

Use this activity to prepare favors for a class party and to demonstrate to children how
an assembly line works.

You need: long table or counter
masking tape
shoe box
toilet-paper tubes (one for each child)
colored tissue paper, pre-cut into
   10″ × 12″ rectangles
transparent tape
ribbon or yarn cut into 8″ lengths (two
   for each child)
two or three margarine tubs
peanuts in shells; small individually
   wrapped pieces of candy; small prizes
   (erasers, stickers, and so on)
holiday stickers
large box, about 15″ × 11″ × 9″

Steps:

1. Set up this assembly-line activity at a long table or counter. Use masking tape to divide the table or counter into seven work areas.

2. Place a shoe box filled with toilet-paper tubes and the tissue paper rectangles in the first area. In the second area, place a roll of transparent tape. Put half of the ribbon or yarn pieces in the third area. In the fourth area, place margarine tubs filled with peanuts in shells, small individually wrapped pieces of candy, and/or small prizes. Place only one kind of treat in each margarine tub. Place the remaining ribbon or yarn pieces in the fifth area. In the sixth area, place holiday stickers. Put a large box in the last area.

3. Select seven children at a time to work at the assembly line. Explain the job of each worker in making the party favors, letting children do the tasks as they are explained:

   First worker—takes a tube from the box, centers it along one short side of a colored tissue paper rectangle, winds the paper around the tube, and hands it to the second worker.

Second worker—tapes the tissue paper in place around the tube and passes it to the third worker.

Third worker—ties a piece of ribbon or yarn around the tissue paper, overlapping one end of the tube, and hands it to the fourth worker.

Fourth worker—fills the tube with a specified number of peanuts, candies, and/or prizes and passes it to the fifth worker.

Fifth worker—ties a piece of ribbon or yarn around the open end of the tissue paper and passes it to the sixth worker.

Sixth worker—places a holiday sticker on the tube and passes it to the seventh worker.

Seventh worker—checks the party favor to see that the ends are tied shut and the paper is taped securely before putting it in the box.

4. Replace the workers with other children every few minutes so that each child has a turn.

CLASS ALBUM OF THE FUTURE
Art and Writing Activity

You need: 9″ × 12″ white construction paper
crayons
pencils
scissors
two pieces of sample wallpaper
hole puncher
yarn scraps
dark marker

Steps:

1. Give each child a 9″ X 12″ sheet of white construction paper. Have children imagine what kind of work they will be doing when they are grown up.

2. Ask each child to decorate the paper with an illustration of him or herself all grown up and working at some occupation.

3. Below the picture, each child will write three or four sentences about his or her future career, telling what he or she likes about the work, how he or she gets to and from work, and why this work is important.

4. To make the front and back covers for the album, trim each of the two pieces of sample wallpaper to 9″ × 12″.

5. Collect the children's papers and punch three holes along the left-hand side of each paper, about ½″ from the edge. Do the same with the front and back covers of the album.

6. Put the papers together between the covers. Thread yarn scraps through the holes and tie in place.

7. Use a dark marker to write *Class Album* on the front cover. Add 20 years to today's date and print the year below the album's title.

Variation:

Have each child select an occupation. He or she can create a collage by cutting out magazine pictures showing tools, products, and people involved in various activities associated with that occupation. Display the collages on a bulletin board.

Look at the pictures of people working in the first box.
Draw a circle around the picture of the work you like best.
Do the same for each of the other boxes.
Turn your paper over and draw a picture of yourself at work.

Name_____

ELVES AT WORK
Worksheet

The elves are working in Santa's workshop. Find six tools that the elves are using. Draw a circle around each tool. Then color the picture.

Name_____

This game will teach children to recognize the materials and equipment
associated with various community helpers.

You need: community-helper cards on this page and game
boards on page 46
glue
oaktag
scissors

Optional: clear plastic adhesive

Steps:

1. Reproduce the community-helper cards on this page nine times.
Make a copy of the game boards on page 46.

2. Mount the cards and game boards on oaktag and laminate them or
cover with clear plastic adhesive.

3. Then cut apart the game boards and cards along the dotted lines.

4. Two to four children may play this game. Have children sit in a
circle on the floor, and give each player a game board. Shuffle the
cards and place them facedown in a pile in the center of the circle.

5. Each player must try to be the first to cover all the pictures on his or
her game board with the appropriate community-helper cards.

6. The youngest child takes the first turn. He or she draws the top card
from the pile and looks to see if his or her game board shows a picture of something associated with that helper. If the child finds a
picture associated with the helper, he or she covers that picture with
the card. If the player's game board does not show a picture of
something associated with the community-helper card, the card is
turned facedown and placed on the bottom of the card pile.

7. The player to the left of the first child then takes a turn. The game
continues clockwise, each player drawing one card per turn. The
first player to cover all the boxes on his or her game board is the
winner.

Variation:

Assign each child one community helper whose equipment and
materials are pictured on his or her game board. The rules of the
game are the same, but each player will cover only the pictures associated with that helper. The first child to cover all three pictures associated with the assigned helper is the winner.

COMMUNITY-HELPERS BINGO
Game Boards

NEIGHBORHOOD HELPERS
Worksheet

Name _____

Along the dotted lines, cut out the pictures of the six helpers at
the sides of the page.
Paste the helpers in the correct boxes in the scenes below.
On the back of your paper, paste the two helpers who are left over.
With crayons, draw pictures to show these two helpers at work.

Children will review important traffic safety rules as they play this game.

You need: pencil
9″ paper plate
red, yellow, and green construction paper
scissors
masking tape

Steps:

1. Trace a 9″ paper plate once onto each color of construction paper; then cut out the three circles. These are the traffic-light signals.

2. Use masking tape to make an intersection on the floor in an open area of the classroom. The width of each "street" should be about 4′. See illustration.

3. Assign one child to be the traffic light. He or she stands in the middle of the intersection, holding the traffic-light signals one by one over his or her head.

4. Choose another child to be the police officer. Ask him or her to stand on a far corner of the intersection.

5. Have the rest of the class line up in a single file. These children are the "cars."

6. Stand on a near corner of the intersection. Motion the first car to approach the intersection. The car will stop next to you. Whisper directions to the car, such as "Turn right," "Go straight," "Go fast," "Go slow," "Turn left."

7. The car must follow the directions, obeying the traffic light.

8. The police officer must watch to see that each car obeys the traffic light. If a car does something the police officer thinks is wrong, the officer must stop the car. The car that was stopped must then repeat the action correctly.

9. After a few minutes, choose other children to be the officer and the traffic light. Play the game for as long as it holds children's interest.

Variation:

Use chalk to mark streets outdoors on the playground. Let some children be pedestrians and have other children be vehicles, using children's riding vehicles if possible. Choose one child to be the police officer. Have him or her direct traffic at the intersection, motioning the vehicles to stop when pedestrians are crossing the street. Let children take turns playing the various roles.

Let children make their own police badges to wear as they act out the roles of police officers
in the "Watch the Traffic Light" activity on page 48.

You need: badge pattern
scissors
pencils
oaktag
black marker
crayons
glue
silver glitter
straight pins

Steps:

1. Reproduce and cut out the badge pattern on this page. Trace it onto oaktag and cut out to make a tracing pattern for children.

2. Have each child trace the badge onto oaktag and cut it out.

3. Ask each child to write his or her name on the badge with a black marker. Assist children if necessary.

4. Next, children will decorate their badges with crayons.

5. To add sparkle to their badges, have children apply thin lines of glue around the edges of the badges and sprinkle silver glitter on the glue. Let dry.

6. Carefully pin a badge on each child's shirt with a straight pin.

Variation:

After children have cut out their oaktag badges, have them wrap aluminum foil around the badges and tape the edges onto the backs of the badges. Ask children to outline their names with glue on the fronts of the badges and press small pieces of yarn onto the glue.

Help the fire engine find the fastest way from the fire station
to the burning house in time to put out the fire!

Name_____

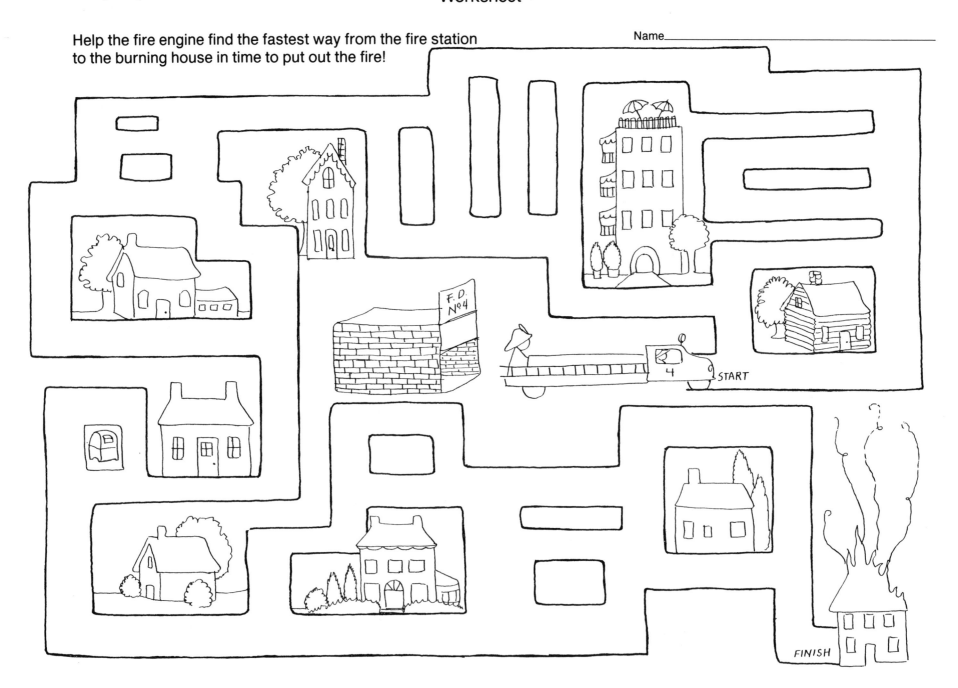

ANIMAL STICK PUPPETS

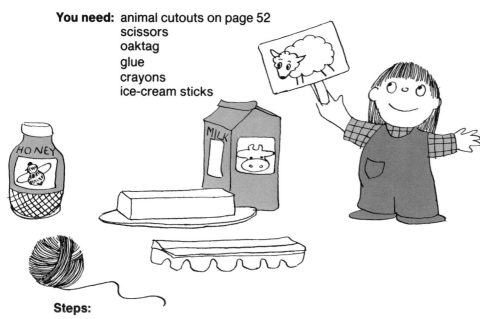

You need: animal cutouts on page 52
scissors
oaktag
glue
crayons
ice-cream sticks

Steps:

1. Use this activity after discussing with children how farmers help us all by caring for animals that supply us with food to eat and material for clothing.

2. Reproduce the animal cutouts on page 52 several times.

3. Let each child choose one animal cutout. He or she will cut it out along the dotted lines and glue it onto a piece of oaktag. The child then trims the oaktag.

4. Next, have children color their animals.

5. Each child will then glue an ice-cream stick onto the back of his or her animal.

6. Slowly read the story on this page to your class. Place emphasis on the underlined words. Every time you mention one of the farmer's animal helpers or the name of something produced by one of the animals, the child holding the indicated puppet will raise it high in the air. For example: "The sheep said . . . " (Children with sheep puppets raise them in the air.)

FARMER BROWN'S ANIMAL HELPERS

One frosty morning, the animals in Farmer Brown's barnyard had an argument about who was the farmer's favorite.

The sheep said, "I give Farmer Brown my soft, fluffy wool so that he can have it made into warm clothes for the winter. I'm his favorite."

"No, you're not!" answered the hen. "Each morning I lay a nice, big egg for Farmer Brown's breakfast. He likes me best."

"Humph!" snorted the cow. "I'm Farmer Brown's favorite—I give him delicious milk to drink. He also makes creamy butter from my milk."

"What about me?" buzzed the bee. "I work hard all summer long making sweet honey for Farmer Brown to eat."

Farmer Brown was just sitting down to his breakfast of toast with butter and honey, scrambled eggs, and milk when he heard all the commotion in the barnyard. He put on his wool hat and coat and went outside to see what was the matter.

"What's all this fuss?" asked Farmer Brown.

"We were arguing about which of us you like best," answered the hen. "Tell us, Farmer Brown."

"Why, you're all my favorites," laughed the farmer. "I wouldn't have much of a farm without cows to give me milk and butter, hens to lay eggs, bees to make honey, and sheep to give me wool. You're the best helpers a farmer could have!" Then Farmer Brown patted the cow and the sheep, clucked to the hen, and winked at the bee before going back to his breakfast.

THE FARMER'S HELPERS
Animal Cutouts

You need: flannel-board characters on
page 54
glue
oaktag
scissors
fine-line markers
felt or flannel scraps
flannel board

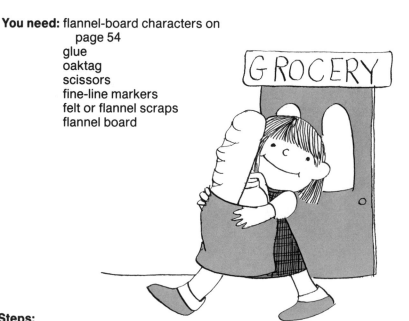

Steps:

1. Begin this activity with a class discussion. Ask several children what they ate for dinner the night before. Then ask them who prepared the meal, and who shopped for the food. Point out that many people help to produce the food we eat.

2. Reproduce the flannel-board characters on page 54.

3. Mount them on oaktag and cut out.

4. With fine-line markers, color the six characters.

5. Glue a small piece of felt or flannel onto the back of each character.

6. Use the characters on the flannel board as you recite the story of "This Is the Bread That Joan Bought."

7. After teaching children the story, let them take turns retelling the story with the flannel-board characters.

Variation:

Give each child a copy of page 54. Have each child color and cut out the characters, and then paste them in order (beginning with Joan) onto a 6″ × 24″ strip of construction paper.

THIS IS THE BREAD THAT JOAN BOUGHT

This is the bread that Joan bought.

This is the grocer who sold the bread that Joan bought.

This is the trucker who delivered the bread to the grocer who sold the bread that Joan bought.

This is the baker who baked the bread that the trucker delivered to the grocer who sold the bread that Joan bought.

This is the miller who ground the wheat that the baker baked that the trucker delivered to the grocer who sold the bread that Joan bought.

This is the farmer who grew the wheat that the miller ground that the baker baked that the trucker delivered to the grocer who sold the bread that Joan bought.

THIS IS THE BREAD THAT JOAN BOUGHT
Flannel-Board Characters

BALING HAY RELAY

You need: masking tape
pipe cleaners
three or four shoe boxes
plastic straws

Steps:

1. Discuss with children the kind of work farmers do. Explain that farmers raise animals such as cows, chickens, and pigs for their meat and for other food products (butter, milk, eggs). Farmers also grow grains and vegetables as food for people and animals. Today farmers use machines to harvest many of their crops. But long ago, farmers had to cut the hay by hand and bundle it together in stacks or bales. After you have finished the discussion, let children play this relay game.

2. Place a 6′ strip of masking tape on the floor, about 5′ in front of a table.

3. Divide the class into three or four equal teams. Ask each team to line up in single file behind the strip of masking tape. Select one child from each team to be a "baler." He or she stands behind the table opposite the team. Give each baler a handful of pipe cleaners.

4. Place a shoe box on the floor beside each team.

5. On the table, spread out lots of plastic straws.

6. At the starting signal, the first player on each team runs to the table and gathers ten straws. He or she then holds the straws while the baler wraps a pipe cleaner around the ten straws to make a "bale of hay." The player then runs back to the team and places the bale of hay in the shoe box before tagging the next player. He or she goes to the end of the line as the next player runs to the table to gather ten more straws in a bundle.

7. The first team to have each player make a bale of hay will sit down. Check the team's bales of hay to see that there are ten straws in each. The team that finishes first and has ten straws in each bale of hay is the winner.

HAYSTACK COOKIES

Ingredients: 12-oz. package of butterscotch chips
12-oz. jar of peanut butter
9-oz. can of chow mein noodles
waxed paper

How to Make:

1. Melt the butterscotch chips in a saucepan over medium heat.

2. When the chips have melted, add the peanut butter and remove from heat. Stir well.

3. Pour in the chow mein noodles. Mix thoroughly.

4. Drop the mixture by spoonfuls onto waxed paper. These will form "haystacks."

5. Let the haystacks harden for about one hour. (Makes three to four dozen haystacks.)

MULTIPURPOSE CAP
Art Activity

Using this cap's basic design, children can make caps to represent those worn
by various members of the community.

NURSE'S CAP

You need: 8½" × 11" white paper
rulers
pencils
scissors
stapler

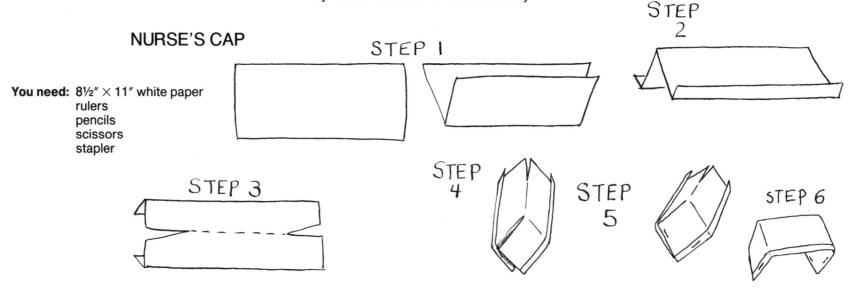

Steps:

1. Give each child an 8½" × 11" piece of white paper. Ask each child to fold the paper in half lengthwise to make a 4¼" × 11" rectangle, as shown.

2. Next, have children unfold their papers and turn them over. Each child will then fold each 11" side up 1". See illustration.

3. With a ruler and a pencil, each child will measure and draw a 3" line along each end of the center crease. See illustration. Then have each child cut along these lines so that each short edge of the paper is divided into two flaps, as shown.

4. Next, each child will pull one flap over the other on one edge of the paper so that the flaps overlap and form a peak. See illustration.

5. Assist children with stapling the overlapped flaps in place. Trim off any excess edges if necessary.

6. Repeat steps 4 and 5 with the opposite edge of the paper to complete the cap.

7. Children will wear their nurses' caps with the short sides over their ears.

Variations:

1. Make an ambulance or emergency medical service worker's cap from white paper. Each child can make a red cross by cutting two 1" × 2" rectangles from red construction paper and gluing them in a cross shape in the center of the front of the cap.

2. Worn with the short sides at the front and back of the head, the nurse's cap becomes a cap for a restaurant worker.

3. To make an army cap, follow the same directions using green construction paper. Have children wear the caps with the short sides at the front and back of their heads. Use blue construction paper to make a navy cap. Have children paint the brims of the caps white. Let children wear their army or navy caps for a Memorial Day class parade.

Read each problem below.
Under each problem, circle the picture of the person who can help you.

Name_____

---

1. You are sick. Who can help you?

2. Your cat is stuck in a tree. Who can help you?

---

3. You are lost. Who can help you?

4. You want to mail a letter to a friend. Who can help you?

---

5. You want to take the bus to school. Who can help you?

6. You want to buy a special birthday cake for a friend.
   Who can help you?

HATS OFF!
Worksheet

The workers on this page have lost their hats.
Help each person find his or her hat.
Cut out the hats in the boxes on the side of the page.
Paste each hat in the box above the correct worker.

Name _____

Have children help prepare these tasty muffins to learn about the work a baker does.

MUFFINS

Ingredients: strawberry jam (see recipe on this
page or use store-bought jam)
1⅔ cups all-purpose flour
¼ cup wheat germ
½ teaspoon salt
2 teaspoons baking powder
¼ cup sugar
2 eggs
2 tablespoons vegetable oil
¾ cup milk

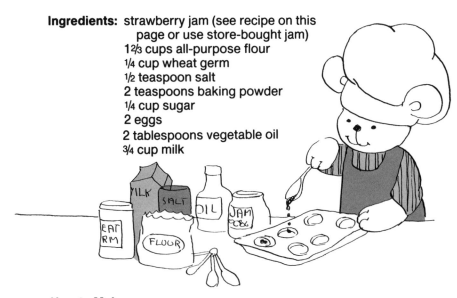

How to Make:

1. In advance, prepare the strawberry jam recipe on this page. (Store-bought jam may be substituted if desired.)

2. Preheat oven to 400°F. Grease muffin tins.

3. In a large bowl, mix together the flour, wheat germ, salt, baking powder, and sugar.

4. In another bowl, beat together the eggs, vegetable oil, and milk.

5. Add the liquid ingredients all at once to the dry ingredients and stir just long enough for the batter to become moist and lumpy.

6. Fill each muffin-tin hole two-thirds full with batter.

7. With a teaspoon, make a slight depression in the batter of each muffin and put a small amount of strawberry jam in it.

8. Bake the muffins for twenty to twenty-five minutes. Cool slightly before serving. Children may spread leftover jam on their muffins before eating them. (Makes about two dozen 2" muffins)

STRAWBERRY JAM

Ingredients: 16-oz.package of frozen
unsweetened strawberries
2 cups sugar
2 tablespoons lemon juice
⅓ cup liquid pectin

How to Make:

1. Thaw the strawberries and pour them into a bowl. Mash them well with a fork.

2. Add sugar and lemon juice to the berries and let stand for one-half hour.

3. Stir in liquid pectin and mix well.

4. Refrigerate mixture for two or three hours or until jam has set. (Makes about two cups of jam.)

Note: Leftover jam from this recipe should not be saved because it may spoil.

Connect the dots from A to Z to see what is in the picture.
Color the picture.
Then turn your paper over and draw a picture of yourself on your way to school.

Name_____

S •

• R

• Q

• B

C •

• Q

• P

• O

D •

• N • M

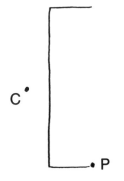

• K • L

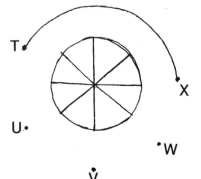

T •

X

• Y

• Z • A

E

F

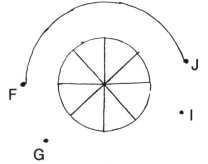

• J

• I

U •

• W

G •

H •

V •

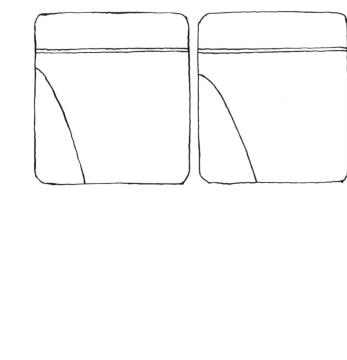

This activity gives children practice in writing letters and in learning about the work of mail carriers.

You need: letter form on page 62
scissors
pencils
scrap paper
small paper bag
crayons
tape
grocery bag

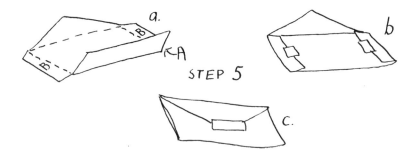

Steps:

1. Reproduce the letter form on page 62 for each child.

2. Have each child cut out the form along the outside black lines.

3. Next, write each child's name on a separate piece of scrap paper. Put the children's names in a small paper bag. Let each child draw a name from the bag. He or she will write a short letter to send to that person, using the lines provided on the letter form.

4. Each child will then draw a picture in the blank box below the writing lines.

5. When children have finished writing and illustrating their letters, show them how to fold the letter forms into envelopes. First, fold the form along the dotted line marked *A* so that the picture and words are covered. See illustration. Next, fold the two side flaps marked *B* along the dotted lines so that they overlap the already

folded section, and secure them with tiny pieces of tape. Then fold the triangular section along the dotted line and tape it in place.

6. Have each child turn over his or her folded form and write on it the name of the person to whom it is being sent.

7. Collect the children's letters and place them in a grocery bag.

8. Select one child to be the mail carrier. He or she will take one letter from the bag, read the name on it, and give the letter to that person. If the child draws a letter addressed to himself or herself, he or she puts it back in the bag and draws another.

9. The child who received the letter becomes the next mail carrier. Continue until all the letters have been delivered.

10. To read their letters, children will untape the top and side flaps and unfold the forms.

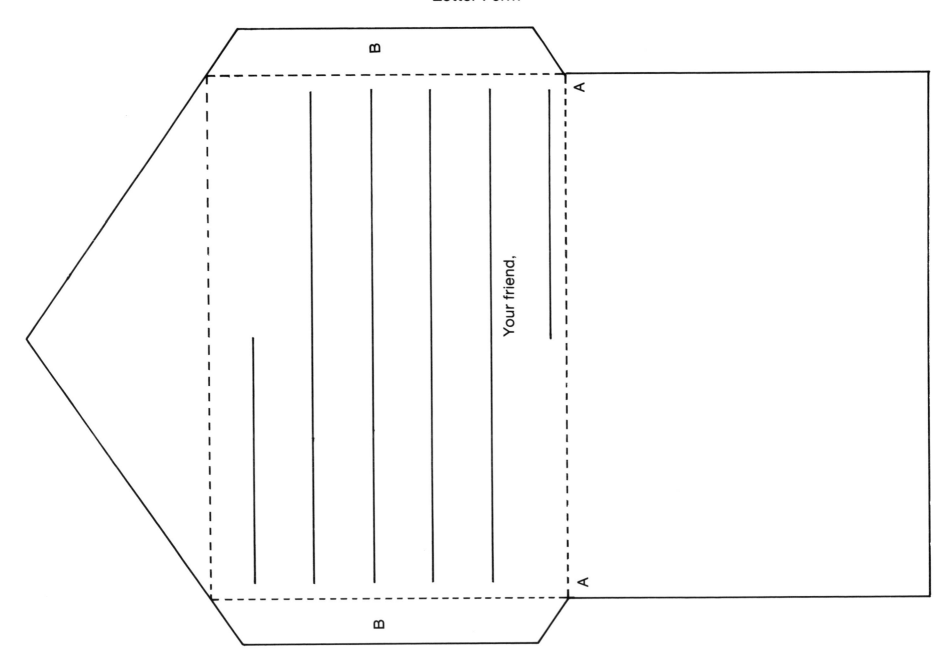

A MAIL CARRIER'S DAY
Worksheet

Name_____

Read the rebus story on this page.
Use the key to help you. Then color the picture of the mail carrier
at the right-hand side of the page.

In the morning, the [mail carrier] goes to the [post office]

The [mail carrier] fills the [mailbag] with [letters]

and [packages]. He or she brings the [letters]

and [packages] to people's homes. If you want to mail

a [letter], you must put it in a [mailbox]. The [mail carrier]

will take your [letter] to the [post office]. Another [mail carrier]

will pick it up from the [post office] and take it to the person's

home.

KEY

mail carrier—   mailbag—   packages—
post office—   letters—   mailbox—

HELPFUL PEOPLE
Suggestions for Using the "Community Helpers" Posters

You need: thumbtacks or pushpins
"Community Helpers" posters included with this unit

Steps:

1. Tack the six "Community Helpers" posters on a bulletin board.

2. Ask individual children to identify the helper on each poster and describe what services that person provides to the community.

3. Then ask the class to imagine what the community would be like without these people. How would the children and their families be affected? Who would do the work of these helpers?

4. Ask children to think of other people whose work benefits many others. Write the children's suggestions on the chalkboard.

5. Next, have individual children stand in front of the class and pantomime the actions of one of the community helpers shown on the posters or listed on the chalkboard. The other children will try to guess which worker is being imitated. The child who guesses correctly then has a chance to pantomime another community helper.

Variations:

1. Have older children write simple descriptions of the work each community helper does. Each child can then read his or her description to the class, letting the other children name the helper being described. The descriptions can then be posted below each poster on the bulletin board.

2. Collect props to symbolize the various helpers: doctor—play stethoscope, bus driver—toy bus, fire fighter—toy fire engine, baker—chef's hat, nurse—nurse's cap, grocer—grocery bag, school crossing guard—safety belt. Hold up the props one at a time and have children name the community helper who uses or wears that item.